Candle Making

IN A WEEKEND

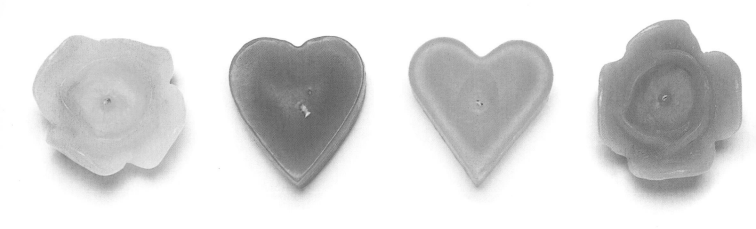

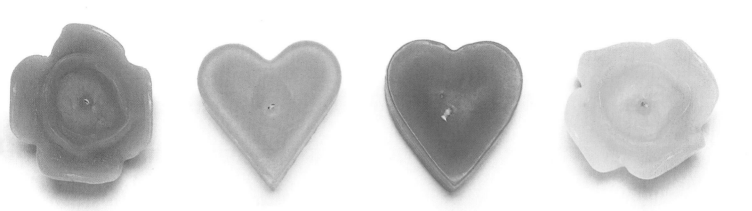

Candle
Making
IN A WEEKEND

Inspirational ideas and
practical projects

SUE SPEAR

TED SMART

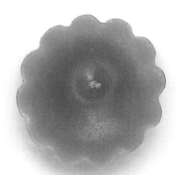

For Amanda and Nicola

This edition published by
The Book People Ltd
Hall Wood Avenue
Haydock
St Helens WA11 9UL

First published in 1999 by
New Holland Publishers (UK) Ltd
London · Cape Town · Sydney · Auckland

2 4 6 8 10 9 7 5 3

ISBN 1 85613 553 5

Editor: Gillian Haslam
Editorial assistant: Anke Ueberberg
Designer: Peter Crump
Photographer: Shona Wood

Editorial Direction: Yvonne McFarlane

Reproduction by PICA Colour Separations, Singapore
Printed and bound in Malaysia by Times Offset (M) Sdn. Bhd.

Important
Every effort has been made to present clear and accurate
instructions. The authors and publishers can accept no liability for
any injury, illness or damage which may inadvertently be caused to
the user while following them.

CONTENTS

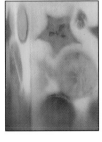

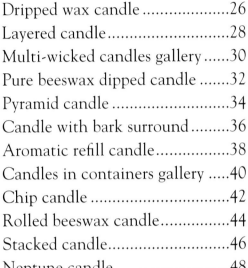

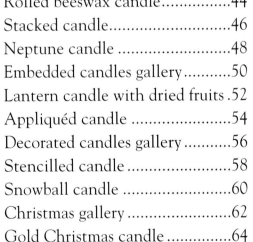

INTRODUCTION 6

A BRIEF HISTORY 8

GETTING STARTED 9

PROJECTS AND GALLERIES 22

Marbled candle 24

Dripped wax candle 26

Layered candle 28

Multi-wicked candles gallery 30

Pure beeswax dipped candle 32

Pyramid candle 34

Candle with bark surround 36

Aromatic refill candle 38

Candles in containers gallery 40

Chip candle 42

Rolled beeswax candle 44

Stacked candle 46

Neptune candle 48

Embedded candles gallery 50

Lantern candle with dried fruits .52

Appliquéd candle 54

Decorated candles gallery 56

Stencilled candle 58

Snowball candle 60

Christmas gallery 62

Gold Christmas candle 64

Garden flare 66

Floating lily 68

Floating hearts 70

Floating candles gallery 72

Carved taper candles 74

Templates 76
Suppliers 78
Acknowledgements 79
Index 80

INTRODUCTION

I have been making candles since 1968 when a friend came to dinner and brought me a hand-made candle rather than a bottle of wine as a gift. In those days candles that were not of the straightforward, single colour, tall and slim variety were not to be seen. Even thicker candles were only used in churches. I was so intrigued with the possibilities of wax that I started to research the subject and to begin making my own candles.

I soon discovered that wax is a marvellous substance to work with. You can dye it wonderful colours, pour it into unusually shaped moulds, perfume it and model with it. The art of making a candle that will burn the way you want it to and also have the colours and effects that you design is very absorbing.

Dining or spending an evening in the warm glow of candlelight is now very much a part of our everyday lives, and the use of aromatherapy oils and other perfumes in wax adds to the charm of candles.

Candles also make wonderful presents. Making your own is far more satisfying than buying something ready-made from a shop, and it is easy to personalize them – either simply by using colours and shapes you know your friends will love, or by decorating them with names, numbers or special messages. In the same way, you can change a basic candle to make something special for occasions such as Christmas, Thanksgiving, Halloween or Valentine's Day.

Candle making is an extremely satisfying hobby. The basic techniques are very simple, and you will probably be able to produce professional-looking candles at your first attempt. It is also relatively inexpensive, and you can recycle both your more unsuccessful efforts and any candle ends. Many people progress from candle making as a hobby to selling candles professionally. Never be afraid to experiment – some of the more thriving candle companies in the world today have based their success on a very simple but innovative candle making idea.

Sue Spear

A BRIEF HISTORY

Before the eighteenth century and the Industrial Revolution, most candles for domestic use were made in the home. They were usually made from tallow, a substance obtained from beef fat. Everyday candles were nothing like the clean burning, smell-free, controlled fires we so enjoy today – they smoked, dripped and smelt revolting. The only quality candles were made from beeswax for the sole use of the churches and the royal family. But even these quality candles would smoke and drip.

With the onset of the Industrial Revolution, longer working hours meant that more sources of light were required and the production of commercial candles began. Fairly sophisticated dipping machines were devised where many wicks were dipped at once and lifted out of the vats of hot wax by a counterweight.

In the early part of the nineteenth century, Michael Chevreul, a French chemist, discovered that tallow contained an important chemical ingredient – stearic acid. Through experiments, he learnt how to separate the stearic acid from the other fatty acids and glycerine also present in the tallow. The result was stearin. The next advance was the extraction of paraffin wax from coal or peat. These two basic ingredients – stearin and paraffin wax – transformed the burning quality of candles. They remain the materials that are still used today, with paraffin wax now obtained as a by-product of refining petrol, and stearin extracted from palm nuts.

The other major improvement in candle making that occurred at the same time was the introduction of plaited cotton wicks. Many different yet inferior materials had been used in the past, including reeds, cloth, thread and string. The idea of plaiting wicks was visionary and a candle made with braided wick burned far more brightly. In fact, Queen Victoria used the new plaited wicks in the candles made for her wedding.

However, the ash produced by the braided cotton was still a problem, causing the candle to smoke excessively. This was resolved in the late eighteenth century when it was discovered that if wicks were first soaked in boric acid, they became self-consuming. If you look closely at a burning candle today you will notice that the wick bends over and the end of the wick is continuously consumed by the flame. This means that no carbon is left on the end of the wick, and the candle burns cleanly.

The mass production of candles began with dipping small batches of candles on frames. This technique is still used, particularly in Scandinavia, and is a development of the technique described in the project on page 32. Other technical advances include compressing powdered wax into shape under great pressure and also extruding wax into long cylindrical poles which are then cut to size. Needless to say, these methods are not suitable for use in the home!

It is rather ironic that it was not until the advent of the use of electricity for lighting that the basic art of candle making was finally perfected. Since then manufacturing techniques have continued to develope – to the joy of those of us who love sitting in the warm glow of a candle flame.

GETTING STARTED

This book clearly describes all the basic techniques you will need for candle making, and also lets you in on the tricks of the trade. Each project in the section that follows not only has a creative idea for you to learn, but also teaches you a basic candle making or decoration technique. If you complete all the projects, you will become an extremely proficient candle maker. Simply start by reading through this chapter thoroughly as it describes all the materials and equipment you will need and explains the basic techniques.

EQUIPMENT

You will need the following basic equipment. You may already have some of it in your kitchen cupboards.

A double saucepan or metal bowl placed over a saucepan of water. If you heat wax directly over the gas or electric ring on your stove, there is a chance it may overheat. This can happen surprisingly quickly and the wax will then catch fire

A wax thermometer (you can also use a sugar thermometer)

A lipped pouring jug

A metal ladle

Kitchen scales – if you are using powdered wax and stearin you can judge the proportion by volume. However, if you are using slab wax you will need to calculate the proportion of wax to stearin by weight

A wicking needle – a huge darning needle that enables you to thread fairly thick wick through small holes in the end of moulds

Wick supports – cocktail or kebab sticks make excellent wick supports

Mould seal – used to seal the base of moulds so the wax does not seep through. You can also use Plasticine

Moulds or containers – see pages 13-15 for more details

The following equipment is not required for all the projects that follow, but will probably come in useful.

Baking trays – several of the projects use baking trays. Using a deep baking tray to place your prepared mould on ensures that if it leaks the wax will not go everywhere

Oven gloves – although wax at 82°C (180°F) is not hot enough to hurt you, it can be more comfortable to use gloves when pouring wax

Craft knife or scalpel – used in several of the projects which follow

Right: A selection of waxes. Clockwise from top left: slab wax, micro soft and micro hard, powder wax, stearin.

MATERIALS

PARAFFIN WAX
Most candles are made from paraffin wax with an additional 10 per cent stearin. Paraffin wax is a by-product of petrol – not as horrid as it sounds when you consider that petrol comes from very old trees!

The wax you buy from suppliers of candle making equipment will already be blended for candle making, and you can buy the stearin either already mixed with the wax or separate.

This type of wax usually melts at about 71°C (160°F). It comes in a variety of forms, either in large 5 kg (11 lb) slabs, or in pellets or powder. The pellets or powder are simpler to use as they are easier to weigh accurately. Buying slabs of wax is generally cheaper, but they have to be broken up first. The easiest way to break a slab of wax is to put it into a large plastic rubbish bag and drop it onto a hard floor.

It is possible to make candles just from paraffin wax. Hand-dipped candles, moulded candles or candles made in rubber moulds do not require

stearin. However, do not use paraffin wax on its own with any type of rigid mould (i.e. moulds made of plastic, metal or glass) as they will be very difficult to get out of the mould. Candles made with paraffin wax without stearin burn slightly quicker, but they also have a translucent appearance and glow very brightly.

ADDITIVES FOR PARAFFIN WAX

STEARIN
Now made from palm nuts, stearin or stearic acid was once obtained from whales, but thankfully animals are no longer used in its production. It has four basic uses and qualities:
• It makes candles easier to get out of the mould – candles contract more when they cool when stearin has been added to the wax.
• Most dyes dissolve more thoroughly in stearin.
• It makes the candle burn longer.
• It makes the candle more opaque, and white candles much whiter.

MICRO SOFT
This is a very soft wax that makes the wax stay soft long enough to mould it. You usually add 10-20 per cent to a quantity of paraffin wax. It is used when you need to keep the wax pliable whilst you mould it (see the floating flower project on page 68).

MICRO HARD
Micro hard wax has a higher melting point than paraffin wax. It can be used in chip candles (see the project on page 42), so ensure that the coloured chips you put into the mould do not melt when the wax is poured over them. It can also be used when embedding wax shapes into the sides of a mould (see the landscape candle in the layered candle project on page 28).

CRYSTAL WAX
This is an over-dipping wax which crystallizes as it cools. See the text on achieving different results on page 18 for more details.

OTHER CANDLE MAKING WAXES

BEESWAX
A wonderful wax which is expensive – but well worth the money. It is available either in blocks or sheets. Blocks are used for melting down. The natural colour of block beeswax is a rich honey brown, but it is also available in bleached form which is better for dyeing ①.

The beeswax sheets can be rolled up to form candles. Beeswax, although long burning, has a very soft consistency and this makes it ideal for rolling. Beeswax sheets are available in a wonderful range of colours.

BAYBERRY WAX
Made from bayberries as its name suggests, this wax is almost impossible to obtain in Europe, but it is available in America where it is traditionally used for Christmas candles.

DIP AND CARVE WAX
This is a specially prepared blend of wax for making dip and carve candles (see page 74). It is much more malleable than paraffin wax and will not crack or splinter when carved.

APPLIQUE WAXES
This soft wax is formed into flat sheets which can be pressed onto a candle's surface, adhering firmly without glue. It is also available in different colours, shapes and numbers ②.

WICKS

Wicks are the most important part of any candle because it is the size of the wick which determines how the candle will burn. Wicks are made from plaited cotton which has been treated with boric acid.

It took hundreds of years to perfect wick making and ironically the final improvements came at about the same

with a pool of wax reaching just to the outside of the candle. Similarly, a candle with a diameter of 2.5 cm (1 in) will need a 2.5 cm (1 in) wick ①.

Professional candle makers classify a wick by the number of strands it contains, for instance a 3/24 wick contains three strands, each made up of 24 smaller strands. It is useful to know this so that you can also count the number of strands if you should lose the wick labels.

- For **dinner candles**, use a wick that approximates as closely as possible the diameter of the candle you are making – usually 1.25 cm (½ in) or 2.5 cm (1 in).
- For **church and block candles**, the wick should be suitable for the diameter of the candle.
- For **cone or pyramid shaped candles**, it is best to opt for a wick size which is suitable for a diameter of about half the width of the candle base. These shaped candles cannot burn perfectly all the way down, but using a wick of this size ensures the candle will burn correctly at first and then leave a shell as it reaches the bottom.
- For **floating candles**, use the correct wick for the diameter of the candle, or use a wick attached to a wick sustainer (see right). Make sure the wick is primed so that it will not draw up water from the base while floating.
- For **refillable candles**, choose a wick much smaller than the diameter of the candle so that it burns down in the middle. You can then refill the candle with a nightlight or powdered wax. A 2.5 cm (1 in) wick is usually adequate for a refillable candle.
- For **container candles**, use a smaller wick than you would use for a free-standing candle. You can buy wax-covered wicks already attached to small metal sustainers which are easy to use.

time as the introduction of electricity. Modern wicks are designed so that they curl over slightly at their tip at the candle burns. This means that the carbon burns off and cannot build up. Before this improvement, carbon would build up, creating smoke, or would fall off, which could be dangerous and a fire risk. Never use string or any other kind of twine for your candles – it really is essential only to use candle wick.

CHOOSING THE RIGHT SIZE OF CANDLE WICK

Candle wick is made from three braided strands. Each strand contains several smaller strands of cotton. Wick sold to amateur candle makers is generally classified by the diameter of the wax the flame will melt as it burns. Therefore, a 5 cm (2 in) candle requires a 5 cm (2 in) diameter wick which will burn

WICK SUSTAINERS

These are small, round metal disks about 1 cm (½ in) in diameter, which hold the wick. You can either buy these on their own or already attached to primed wick for container candles.

PRIMED WICK

This is wick that has been put into molten wax, taken out immediately and then straightened. This stiffens it and is useful for some candle-making methods. It is also good to prime the wick that will protrude from the finished candle as it make the candle easier to light. Wicks for floating candles should always be primed so they do not draw up water ②.

TROUBLESHOOTING

If the wick is just slightly too small, the candle will drip. When making wider candles, if the wick is much too small it will burn down the middle of the candle. If this happens, save the candle and refill it.

If the wick is too large, the candle will burn with a large flame and will smoke. Even one faulty candle can produce a large amount of smoke which can ruin a room's decoration. This can be avoided by cutting off surplus wick as it burns.

Having chosen the correct wick, it is very important to position the wick securely in the centre of the candle. If the wick leans to one side, the candle will drip and burn very quickly and could be dangerous. If making candles in glass containers, the glass will crack if the flame touches the side.

CANDLE MOULDS

It is now possible to buy a large variety of ready-made candle moulds ③. These come in a variety of forms:

PLASTIC MOULDS

These are available in both clear plastic (which is useful when you need to see what you are doing) and opaque plastic. They are easy to use and will last for a great many candles if handled with care. They produce professional results, but temperature control is essential as

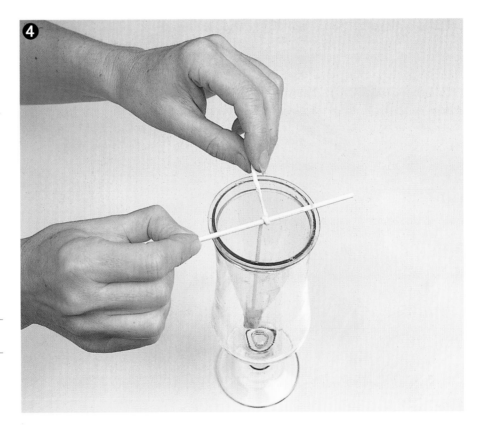

the moulds may melt if pouring in wax that has been heated above 82°C (180°F) ④. A plastic mould has been used in the shell project on page 48.

METAL MOULDS

Metal moulds are similar to plastic, but they last forever. They have the added

advantage in that they will not buckle if extremely hot wax is poured in.

LATEX MOULDS

Latex moulds are used when you want to make a candle in a particular shape. To use them, thread the wick in through the tip of the mould using a wicking

⑤

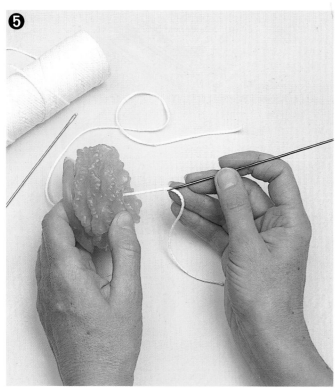

⑥

needle ⑤. Then coat the inside of the mould with mould release, pour in the wax and support the mould in a suitable container while the wax cools ⑥.

You can make you own latex moulds of a chosen object using liquid latex and a non-porous master. Here we have used an orange ⑦.

First wash the orange or chosen object in hot soapy water to remove any grease. Place the orange on a

surface such as an old plate. Following the manufacturer's instructions, mix the latex with a little thickener. Using a brush, paint the latex over the object. You will need to apply several layers in order to build the latex up to a thickness of 3 mm (⅛ in). Allow the latex to dry until it is just sticky between coats. The mould should be left to dry overnight before peeling off the master.

All kinds of household objects make very satisfactory candle moulds. Try using milk or yoghurt cartons for block candles, bun tins or chocolate moulds for small floating candles, or large cake tins for multi-wicked candles. Take a look around your kitchen and you will be surprised at how many kitchen objects can be adapted. If using old plastic containers take care not to pour in wax over 82°C (180°F) ⑧.

CARDBOARD MOULDS
A cardboard mould is used for the project on page 34. Cardboard is ideal for making candles when the wax is poured in at a very cold temperature, producing a white, scaly effect. If you try to make candles like this in an ordinary mould, you may not be able to remove them from the mould as they may not have contracted enough.

OPEN ENDED MOULDS
It is possible to make candles in a mould which does not have a base. The floating candles on page 70 made with cake cutters show one method. Alternatively, you can surround the base of the mould with mould seal and then pour in the wax.

To position the wick when using open ended moulds, either stick it to

⑦

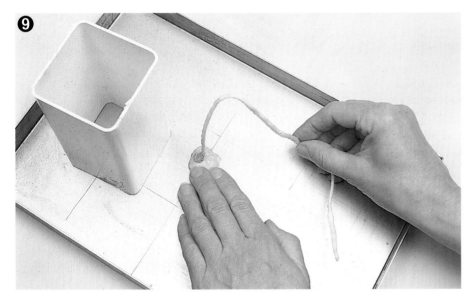

expensive and are only sold in large quantities. Dyes come in two forms.

DYE DISCS

These are dyes that have already been dissolved in some stearin. Even so, you will ensure that you get the most out of your dye disc by dissolving some of it yourself in stearin first. These dyes are very concentrated – one dye disc will usually dye about 2 kg (4½ lb) of wax. It is easy to cut pieces off with a sharp knife, so you do not have to use the whole disc at once.

POWDERED DYES

Powdered dyes are extremely strong. A portion the size of a match-head will colour about 1 kg (2¼ lb) of wax. All powdered dyes must be dissolved in heated stearin first or you will be left with dark spots in the candle and waste the dye. Powdered dyes can also be messy and have to be used with great care, as the powder can get everywhere if spilt. The dye will stain even if it is spilt when dry and some colours are very difficult to remove.

CALCULATING HOW MUCH DYE TO USE

Obviously this is very much to do with your personal taste. However, remember it is always possible to make a colour darker or brighter by gradually adding more dye. Making a candle lighter is much more problematic as you have to add more wax – sometimes

your worksurface with mould seal, or make a hole in a piece of wood or stiff card, thread the wick through and seal it underneath with mould seal in the usual way ⑨.

DYES

Always use dyes which are prepared especially for candle making ①. They come in a wonderful variety of colours which can be mixed. Dyes will fade if they are exposed to sunlight – especially the pink and red shades – so be sure to keep your finished candles away from direct sunlight. You can buy pigments which do not fade, but they are more

very much more than you want. So always add to a pale colour until you get used to the potency of the dye you are using.

PREPARING DYED WAX FOR OVER-DIPPING

When a candle is dipped in a different colour once it has been made, the proportion of dye to wax will have to be much larger. Because you are relying on a very thin layer of wax to change the colour, the dyed wax has to be very strong. Experiment by gradually adding more dye until you have the over-dip colour you need.

MIXING CANDLE DYE COLOURS

Candle dyes mix very easily but not always predictably. Experiment with small quantities first, and don't be afraid to use strange combinations. The usual rules of colour combinations do not always apply. For example, orange and pink mixed together make a bright Christmassy red.

PERFUMES

One of the wonderful qualities of wax is how well it absorbs perfume. A burning candle functions just like an atomiser. The molten pool of warm wax at the top of the candle gently heats the perfume which rises and permeates the atmosphere. The larger the pool of molten wax, the more effective the scent will be. This is why container candles which create a comparatively large pool of molten wax are ideal for perfume candles, and dinner candles, which have a very small diameter, the least effective.

As with other candle ingredients, it is essential that you use only scents which have been especially designed for candles. It can be dangerous to use other perfumes as the perfume must be oil-based and mixed with a 'carrier' only suitable for candle use. Other perfumes may, at worst, flare up or leave the wick clogged with carbon.

HOW MUCH TO USE

This depends on how strong you want the scent to be, and of course some

perfumes are more pervasive than others. However, most reasonably strongly scented candles contain about 6 per cent of perfume to wax. The easiest way to judge this is by weight. You can put as much as 10 per cent in but this makes a very strongly perfumed candle which may be overpowering.

HOW PERFUMES AFFECT COLOUR

Only make up small batches of perfumed wax to begin with as they can affect the candles' colour. Some perfumes already have a slight colour of their own and their use can, for instance, change a white candle to ivory.

DIFFERENT SCENTS AND THEIR USES

You can use different scents to for different functions. All aromatherapy scents are available in candle perfumes, as is citronella (for repelling insects). Other special uses include smoke-repelling scents (usually a sweet smelling perfume like rose – all candles help to absorb cigarette smoke).

MAKING A BASIC CANDLE

PREPARE THE MOULD

Take a length of wick twice the length of the mould. Prime the tip by dipping it into hot wax. Using a wicking needle, thread the wick through the hole at the top of the mould and seal it with mould seal. Press it down well. (This is not necessary if you are using rubber moulds as they seal themselves). Thread a cocktail stick through the wick at the base so that it is centred in the middle of the mould.

SUPPORT THE MOULD

Use a roll of cardboard, cup, jug or anything else you can find to do the job.

WEIGH THE WAX AND STEARIN

With practice you will be able to judge how much wax you will need for your finished candle. A good rough guide is to weigh a ready-made candle of approximately the same size as the mould you are going to use. When you have decided the total weight needed,

subtract 10 per cent. Weigh out this amount (i.e. 10 per cent) of stearin. Weigh out 90 per cent of the total weight in wax.

HEAT THE STEARIN IN A DOUBLE SAUCEPAN

You could also use a bowl placed over a saucepan of hot water. The stearin has completely melted when it has turned into a clear liquid.

ADD THE DYE TO THE MELTED STEARIN

Judging the right amount of dye to use is also easier with experience. However, don't worry if the colour is not strong enough. You can always heat up a little more stearin and add more dye later. It will not matter if the candle contains more than 10 per cent stearin.

ADD THE WAX

Add the wax to the stearin and dye mixture and heat in the double saucepan until it is all melted.

ADD THE PERFUME

Add perfume to the wax (if you are making a scented candle), and then gently stir.

TEST THE TEMPERATURE OF THE WAX

Heat the wax to 82°C (180°F). Make sure that you stir the wax gently before taking its final temperature. Leave the thermometer in the wax until it has stopped rising. It is very important that you do not overheat the wax as there is a possibility that it could catch fire.

FILLING A PREPARED MOULD

Warm the dipping jug with hot water – if it is too cold it will alter the temperature of the wax. Then ladle the wax into the jug and pour gently into the mould creating as little turbulence as possible. Leave some wax in the saucepan for 'topping up'.

TOPPING UP

While the wax cools, it contracts and the wax sinks. Wait until a thick skin has formed on the top of the wax and then pierce it with a pencil or wicking needle. Make sure you prod the surface properly or you may be left with holes in the finished candle! Then pour in some more wax also heated to 82°C (180°F), being very careful that the wax is not too hot (it may crack the candle), too cold (it will not adhere to candle) or that you do not fill it over the original level of the candle (making it difficult to get out of the mould). You may have to top up more than once before the final surface is flat.

It is always surprising how much a candle contracts and less experienced makers often underestimate how much extra wax they will need for this stage. As you usually make candles upside down (you are 'topping up' what will become the bottom of the candle), you can top up with a different coloured wax if necessary.

REMOVE THE CANDLE FROM THE MOULD
The candle must be left until it is completely cold before removing it from the mould. This can vary from a few hours to overnight, depending on the size of the candle and the wax used. When properly set, the candle should come out easily from the mould when you pull it.

OTHER CANDLE MAKING TECHNIQUES

As well as moulding candles, there are two other techniques that can be used. The first, and most traditional, is hand-dipping. This is fully explained in the project on page 32.

The second, and more unusual, is rolling. This is illustrated in the project on page 44, using beeswax sheets. However, the same basic method can

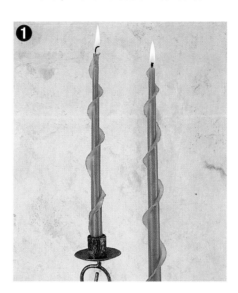

be used with paraffin wax mixed with 20 per cent micro soft which has been poured into a tray and left to just set. The wax is then lifted out of the tray and rolled. The rolled wax candle shown here has been made with a triangular piece of wax rolled around a wick ①. The pretty foliating edges have been made simply by squeezing the edges and turning them outwards.

MAKING CANDLES IN CONTAINERS

You do not have to make candles in moulds. It is really easy to make candles in containers and many of the most unlikely objects can make really attractive candles. The method is demonstrated in the project on page 38.

The photograph here shows some ideas, but almost any container made of ceramic, metal or glass can be used ②. Use terracotta pots of varying sizes for garden candles. Shells, coconut shells, household tins, glasses, vases and even egg shells can all be used. Although it can only be used once, hollowed out fruit is also a possibility.

ACHIEVING DIFFERENT EFFECTS AFTER THE CANDLE HAS SET

OVER-DIPPING IN CLEAR WAX
If you have made a candle and you do not like its final finish, for instance if you have used an open ended mould and the top looks a bit rugged, you can over-dip the candle for a different effect. Dip the candle in clear wax heated to about 88°C (190°F) and then into water. This will smooth out any deficiencies and make the candle shiny.

OVER-DIPPING IN DIFFERENT COLOURED WAX
Using very strongly dyed wax, a candle can be dipped into a can of wax and its colour changed completely. The same principle can be used to make pretty designs on candles. Different colours can be poured over the candle to completely change its appearance. The candle illustrated has had blue wax poured over it, followed by a complete over-dip in green. The over-dipping wax should be kept at a temperature of about 77°C (170°F) ①.

OVER-DIPPING OR SPLASHING WITH CRYSTALLINE WAX
Crystalline wax forms little crystals as it cools. It looks extremely effective if carefully splashed or poured over a coloured candle ②.

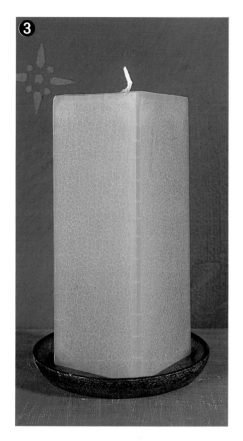

OVER-DIPPING IN ICE COLD WATER
If you dip the candle in uncoloured wax heated to 88°C (190°F) and then plunge it immediately into a bucket of ice cold water, a square crystal formation will decorate the outside of the candle ③.

HAMMERING
Using a round headed hammer you can build up a pattern of white edged craters around the candle ⑤.

SANDPAPERING
Gently rub the candle, either using a very fine sandpaper, which gives an almost silken finish, or a coarser sandpaper, which gives the candle a more rustic appearance ④.

EMBEDDING OBJECTS
There are two basic methods for embedding objects into the sides of candles. The first, and simplest, is to use wax glue. This is shown in the project on page 36. The second method is to soften the outside of the candle by immersing it in a bath of warm wax until it is soft, then take it out and press the objects into the soft exterior ⑥.

You can also dip the finished candle into clear wax, just to fix the items, such as appliquéd numbers or letters, a little more firmly. If this final dip covers up the objects too much, carefully scrape away the excess from the surface of the decorations.

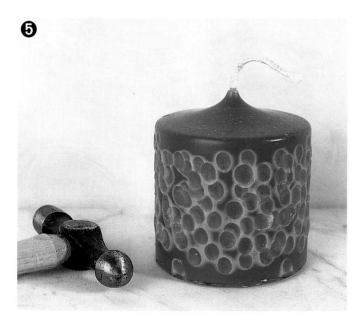

CANDLE VARNISH
This is a special varnish that will give the candle a hard surface and a brilliant shine. It should be painted onto the candle using a soft brush. Varnish has been used in the project on page 74.

GOLD AND SILVER WAX
This rub-on coloured wax is easy to use and produces very satisfying results.

POSTER PAINTS
These paints can be used to decorate candles. Dilute them slightly with washing-up liquid to make them easier to apply. You can also experiment with other types of paint – the general rule is that water-based paint will adhere to wax successfully.

FELT-TIPPED PENS
It is well worth experimenting with felt-tipped and metallic pens. Some brands can be used on candles very successfully, whilst others do not produce good results.

HEART-PATTERNED CANDLE
This candle has been decorated by dipping a candle twice into a can of wax that has been dyed red. While the wax is still warm, use a cake cutter to remove the heart shape from the red wax, leaving a white heart exposed ⑦.

HOW TO BURN CANDLES SAFELY AND CLEANLY

POSITIONING CANDLES
Ensure candles are placed safely in your room. They should be put well away from other objects. Be especially careful not to put them on shelving where they might light the shelf above. Do not place candles where dripping wax could cause damage. Candle wax is very difficult to remove from the inside of televisions!

CHOOSING CANDLE HOLDERS
It is important that any candle holder you use should sit steadily and that it is not made from inflammable materials.

NEVER LEAVE A CANDLE UNATTENDED
It is extremely dangerous to leave burning candles unattended. Always make sure that all candles are extinguished if you leave the room and take extra care if there are young children present.

KEEP THE WICK TRIMMED
Sometimes the wick on a candle becomes too long and the candle begins to smoke. If the flame is not rounded but flares out at the top, the wick needs trimming. You can trim the wick with a pair of scissors whilst it is still burning.

KEEP THE WICK CENTRED
In larger diameter candles the wick does not always go straight down the middle. Keep an eye on it and if it appears to be on one side, push it into the centre again using a small stick or match stick.

POSITION OUT OF A DRAUGHT
No candle will burn well when it is placed in a draught. Always place your candles in sheltered positions.

GET THE MOST OUT OF THE CANDLE FLAME
If you want the most light from your candles, place them in front of mirrors so the light is reflected ①.

❶

• If you do have a fire, do not use water to put it out. Wax fires should be treated the same way as an oil fire. You should switch off the heat source and then smother the flames with a saucepan lid, damp cloth or with a special fire blanket.

WORKING CLEANLY

Always wear an apron when candle making. If you do get any wax on your clothes, place some tissue or newspaper over the wax and run a hot iron over it. Keep doing this until no more wax appears on the paper.

Try and work in such a way that the potential problem of wax spillage is minimised. It is a good idea to cover your kitchen surface with newspaper before you start. Also, for added security, place your prepared candle moulds in a deep baking tray to catch the wax in case the mould leaks. Holding a tray under the jug as you pour minimises the drips.

If you do spill wax, it will usually come off a kitchen surface quite easily when it has cooled. A paint scraper or spatula is the easiest implement for this.

Be very careful never to pour wax down the kitchen sink as it will harden and block the drain. If this happens, try pouring boiling water down the sink. If that fails, call a plumber. If you are making candles near the sink, it is safer simply to put the plug in.

Keep your moulds and equipment clean. In most cases the wax will come out of its container easily when it contracts. If you are left with a wax residue, wash the container in very hot soapy water, making sure that you keep the hot tap running and that only a little wax goes down the plug hole.

White spirit is an excellent cleaner and will dissolve small drops of wax. One word of caution – some of the dyes, particularly pink and purple, are very powerful and if they come into contact with plastic it is almost impossible to get them out.

Foil containers and bowls are excellent for keeping pieces of leftover wax. You can also use them for topping up and for chip candles.

CANDLE HINTS AND TIPS

REFILLING A REFILLABLE CANDLE

When using a candle that is designed to burn down the middle and then be refilled with a nightlight or wax when a well has formed, it is important that you burn it correctly to create the well. Light the candle and burn until the wax has melted to a diameter of about 4.5 cm (1¾ in). When the pool of wax is about 3 mm (⅛ in) deep, extinguish the candle and pour out the molten wax. Re-light the candle and trim the wick. Repeat these steps until the candle has burnt down far enough to refill with a nightlight or wax ①.

PLACING A CANDLE ON A METAL SPIKED HOLDER

If you push a candle down directly onto a spiked holder it may split. To avoid this, heat the spike with a match or cigarette lighter flame before you push the candle onto it.

PUTTING CANDLES IN THE FRIDGE

Leave your candles in the fridge for several hours before you burn them. This will harden the wax and they will burn longer. This is particularly useful if you live in a very warm climate.

HOW TO PUT CANDLES OUT

When extinguishing a container candle, a refillable candle or any candle where a large well of wax has melted in the middle, never simply blow the candle out. The wick may well sink into the molten well and be impossible to retrieve when you want to re-light the candle. Instead, using a match stick or pencil, push the wick down into the wax, and then lift it up again so it is ready for re-lighting.

WORKING SAFELY

Candle making is a safe and enjoyable hobby, but wax will ignite when it is overheated so it is essential that you follow these guidelines.

If wax is heated above 100°C (212°F) it will ignite, so:
• Never leave heating wax unattended.
• Always heat the wax over indirect heat. Use either a double saucepan with the bottom half filled with water and wax in the top half or a bowl over a saucepan of hot water.
• Make sure the water does not boil dry.

PROJECTS AND GALLERIES
FOR MAKING CANDLES

MARBLED CANDLE

This easy project shows how a simple, plain candle can be dipped several times in coloured wax and transformed into a jewel-like object using a creative marbling technique.

1 Dip the prepared candle once into the heated pink wax. Set aside and allow the wax to cool – this should only take 2-3 minutes. Repeat the dipping process while the wax is hot if you are making more than one candle.

YOU WILL NEED

7.5 cm (3 in) round ball candle
Container of pink wax, heated to 85°C (185°F) ready for dipping
Container of chalky white wax, heated to 85°C (185°F) ready for dipping
Container of blue wax, heated to 85°C (185°F) ready for dipping
Container of clear wax, heated to 85°C (185°F) ready for dipping
Sharp knife
Potato peeler
Bowl of cold water

TIP
REFILLING THE CANDLE
Burn the candle for an hour or until the wax has burnt to a diameter of 3 cm (1¼ in). Blow out the candle and pour in more molten wax. Repeat until you have a hole in the candle about 2 cm (¾ in) deep. Either refill this with a nightlight or some powdered wax and a wick.

2 Now dip the candle three times in white wax, three times in blue wax, then a further three dips in white wax and one last dip in pink wax. Allow the candle to cool slightly between each dipping.

3 Using a sharp knife, cut a section off the bottom of the candle so that it will stand safely. You may need to scrape some wax off to ensure the base is flat and even.

4 Using both your thumbs, press firmly down all around the circumference of the candle to create little craters or indentations.

5 Using a sharp potato peeler, gently begin to shave pieces off the surface of the candle. Work horizontally at first, almost as if you are peeling an orange, then work evenly up and down the surface of the candle.

6 Continue carving the candle's surface until you have created a pleasing effect by exposing enough of the underlying colours. You may have to shave off quite a lot of wax to achieve this.

7 Check that the temperature of the clear wax is at 85°C (185°F). Suspend the candle in the hot wax. The rough edges will melt off, and slightly more layers will become exposed. Remove the candle from the wax as soon as you have achieved the desired effect. Finally, dip the candle in cold water to give it a good shine.

DRIPPED WAX CANDLE

Any candle made with a wick that is too small will drip. This 'defect' can be used to your advantage with this project, where the candle is deliberately designed to drip wax in a variety of colours. The wax cascades down the sides of the candle, producing this pretty effect.

1 Holding the candle by the wick, dip it into the red wax and then into water. Repeat this three times.

YOU WILL NEED

A ready-made 25 cm (10 in) candle

A dipping can filled with red paraffin wax, heated to 79°C (175°F)

A dipping can filled with blue paraffin wax, heated to 79°C (175°F)

A dipping can filled with green paraffin wax, heated to 79°C (175°F)

A dipping can filled with yellow paraffin wax, heated to 79°C (175°F)

A dipping can filled with ivory paraffin wax, heated to 79°C (175°F)

Container of water

Scalpel or craft knife

VARIATIONS

You can also make this candle by pouring the wax over the candle.
This means that you will have to prepare far less wax.

2 Dip the candle into the can of blue wax and then into the can of cold water. Repeat three times.

3 Dip the candle into the green wax and then into water. Repeat three times. Then continue in the same way with four dips in yellow wax and finally four dips in ivory wax.

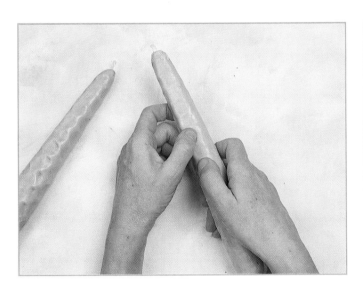

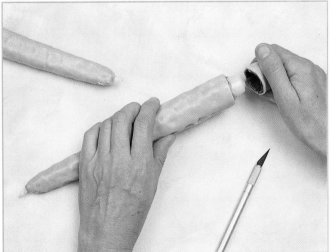

4 Using your fingers, press firmly against the candle to make small indentations all the way around the candle. Place the candle in cold water to cool.

5 Using a craft knife, score a circle around the base of the candle and gently pull off the coloured layers of wax so that the candle will fit into the neck of the bottle.

LAYERED CANDLE

The colours of this candle blend into each other to produce a simple yet effective finish. This basic technique can take a while to master as each layer must be poured in at the right time and at the right temperature.

1 Set up the mould. Heat all four waxes separately until they are molten. Heat the turquoise wax to 82°C (180°F) and pour gently into the mould to a depth of 1 cm (½ in). Try to avoid splashing the sides. Make a hole in the centre and position the wick. Twist the top of the wick around a stick to support it.

YOU WILL NEED

Candle mould
100 g (4 oz) blue paraffin wax and stearin mix
100 g (4 oz) turquoise paraffin wax and stearin mix
100 g (4 oz) pink paraffin wax and stearin mix
100 g (4 oz) lilac paraffin wax and stearin mix
Wax thermometer
20 cm (8 in) length of 5 cm (2 in) primed wick
Stick, to support wick
Soft cloth or duster

TIP

Make sure that the temperature has been accurately read before you pour. If it is too hot, the colours will mix; too cold and you will get a white ridge around the join.
If the candle is not perfect enough to polish, don't despair. A final dip in wax at 88°C (190°F) will cover up a multitude of sins.

2 Wait until the turquoise wax is completely set around the edge, but still very soft to the touch in the middle. Heat the lilac wax to 82°C (180°F) and pour in another layer 1 cm (½ in) deep.

3 Continue in the same manner with the blue and then the pink wax. Then repeat steps one and two and finally add a thin layer of blue wax. Give the candle a final top up.

4 Leave the candle until completely cold and then carefully remove from the mould.

5 To finish off, polish the layered candle with a soft cloth or duster.

--- VARIATIONS ---

Tipping the mould at different angles when you pour in the wax also produces some interesting effects when the colours set at varying angles.

PURE BEESWAX DIPPED CANDLE

This project explains the earliest form of candlemaking – hand-dipping. Although time-consuming, hand-dipped candles burn beautifully and no wax is better suited to this technique than pure beeswax.

1 Heat the wax until it has all melted. Measure out a length of wick and hold it in the middle. Dip both ends of the wick into the beeswax, and then remove. Repeat the dipping three times.

TIP
If possible, it may help to make these candles in a dipping can placed in a saucepan on the stove. Because so many dips are involved, the wax may form a skin several times and have to be re-heated before the candles are finished.

2 Continue dipping the ends of the wick until the coating of wax becomes thicker. This hand-dipping means you will end up with candles that are much thicker than those produced commercially.

3 After approximately 30 dips you will have an ordinary sized pair of candles, similar to the standard ones available in shops.

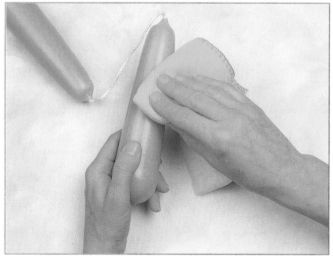

4 Continue dipping, reheating the wax as necessary. Stop when the candles have reached a diameter of 4 cm (1½ in) at the base.

5 Dip the candles immediately into cold water to produce a final shine. When dry, you can also buff them with a soft cloth.

PYRAMID CANDLE

This project illustrates how easy it is to make candles in cardboard moulds. This candle uses a pyramid shape, but is it just as simple to make squares and cylinders. The mould is thrown away after use, so it can simply be torn off the candle. The coldness of the wax gives it its scaly appearance.

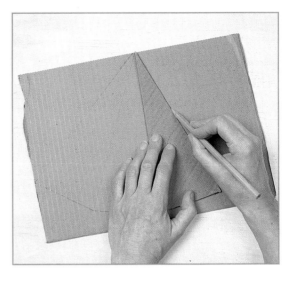

1 Using the smaller piece of cardboard, cut out a triangular template 9.5 cm (3¾ in) across the base and 21 cm (8½ in) along the sides. Cut out the template. On the large piece of cardboard, draw around the template four times to make a fan shape as shown. Alternatively copy the template on page 76.

YOU WILL NEED

A sheet of cardboard 15 x 23 cm (6 x 9 in)

A sheet of cardboard 30 x 23 cm (12 x 9 in)

Pencil

Scalpel or craft knife

Metal ruler

Brown tape

Scissors

20 cm (8 in) of 4 cm (1½ in) primed wick

Wicking needle

Stick, to support the wick

Tall container (see step 5)

250 g (9 oz) orange wax

25 g (1 oz) stearin

Double saucepan

─── **TIP** ───

Pouring in cold wax is possible when using a cardboard mould as the mould can be torn off the set candle and it does not matter if the candle sticks to the sides.

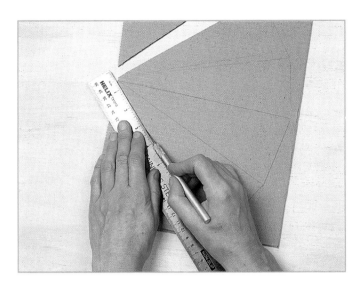

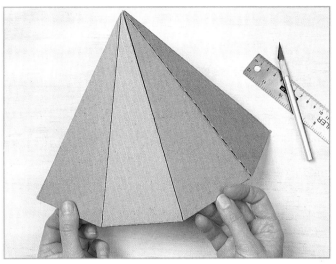

2 Cut out around the outside of the fan shape using the craft knife and metal ruler and discard the trimmings.

3 Score down the lines of the diagonals using the ruler and craft knife. Score just deep enough to bend the board, taking care not to cut right through the board.

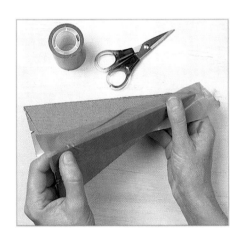

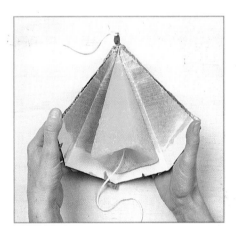

4 Fold the shape into a pyramid shape and tape the two edges together with a strip of brown tape.

5 Using a wicking needle, thread the wick through the centre of the mould and out through the taped, pointed end. Turn the mould upside down, place a stick across the base and bend the wick over. Place the cardboard mould into a tall container for support. Heat the prepared orange wax and stearin mix to just 71°C (160°F) and pour into the mould. Pierce the surface and top up in the usual way.

6 When the candle is completely cold, peel off the cardboard to reveal your candle. Remember that the top of the wick is secured by the brown tape, so take care not to break off the top of the candle.

CANDLE WITH BARK SURROUND

Natural bark is used to wonderful effect in this unusual woodland candle. Wax glue is used to fix the bark to the candle and because a small wick is used, the candle can be re-filled several times.

1 Using the hacksaw and protecting the work surface if necessary, cut the bark into lengths of approximately 5 cm (2 in).

— TIP —

Because this candle uses a wick size which is so much smaller than the diameter of the candle it is quite safe. You can also refill it with a nightlight or powdered wax and primed wick when it has burnt down about 2.5 cm (1 in).

2 Heat the wax and stearin mixture until it reaches a temperature of 82°C (180°F) and pour into the solid-based cake tin.

3 Wait until the wax has nearly cooled and then insert a length of primed wick. Push it down until it reaches the bottom. Then lift it up 3 mm (⅛ in) so that it will not burn right down to the bottom when alight.

4 Support the wick with a wick support resting across the cake tin. Then top up the candle with more wax. Leave to cool.

5 When completely cold, remove the candle from the cake tin. Apply a liberal amount of wax glue to the bark strips and press them against the side of the candle.

AROMATIC REFILL CANDLE

Candle perfumes can be used for many purposes, from soothing aromatherapy to practical smoke repelling. Burning them in a glass makes sure there is a pool of molten wax. This is essential if the perfume is to become atomised and permeate the surroundings.

1 Prepare wax, dye and perfume mix (see pages 15-16). Heat the wax to a temperature of 82°C (180°F). Pour into the base of the tumbler to a depth of about 4 mm (¼ in). Wait until it has almost set and then push the wick and sustainer down into the soft wax. Use a skewer or wicking needle to help push the sustainer down.

YOU WILL NEED

100 g (4 oz) paraffin wax
Dye in a colour of your choice
6-8 g (⅛-¼ oz) candle perfume
Double saucepan
Wax thermometer
Glass tumbler
Length of 10 cm (4 in) primed wick
Wick sustainer
Stick, to support the wick
Skewer or wicking needle
Cocktail stick

TIP

Make sure the wick is properly centred. If the flame touches the sides, it will break the glass.

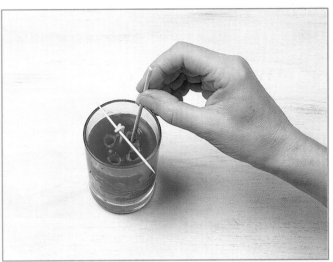

2 Place a cocktail stick across the top of the tumbler and twist the wick around it. Pour in the wax and perfume mix to within 1 cm (½ in) of the top of the tumbler.

3 When the candle is half set, pierce the top of the wax in several places using the skewer or needle.

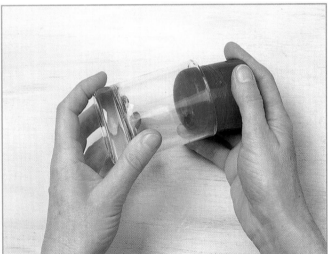

4 Leave until the candle is almost cold then top up with the remaining wax. Try not to top up over the original level of wax – this will make it easier for the candle to drop out of the glass.

5 Turn the glass upside down and remove the candle from the glass. You now have the glass free to make more refills.

CANDLES IN CONTAINERS GALLERY

CHIP CANDLE

This candle uses chips of different colours inside the candle to give the multicoloured, geometric effect. Chip candles are an ideal way to use up leftover pieces of wax from other projects, and have the added advantages that they set quickly and are fast to make.

1 To create the chips, heat the purple wax to 82°C (180°F) and pour into a tray. Wait until the wax has cooled, and then cut up into tiny squares. Repeat with pink wax.

YOU WILL NEED

10 purple and 10 pink wax chips
(see step 1)

Wax thermometer

Baking tray

A cone mould

15 cm (6 in) length of 4 cm (1½ in)
primed wick

Stick, to support the wick

100 g (4 oz) orange wax and
stearin mix

Dipping can of clear wax, for
over-dipping

TIP

Chip candles need little topping up as the amount of molten wax added to the mould is very small – most of the candle is set before the wax is poured in.

2 Set up a cone candle mould. Place
the chips into the mould, against
the sides if possible. Make sure that the
wick remains placed in the centre of
the mould.

3 Heat the orange wax to 82°C
(180°F). Pour it into the mould.
Wait until the candle has completely
set and then remove it from the mould.

4 Heat a container of wax to 85°C
(185°F). Pour into a dipping can
and holding the candle by the wick, dip
it until the colour of the chips has
become exposed.

5 Warm a baking tray in the oven,
then remove to a heat-resistant
surface. Put the candle upright on the
tray and push down gently to melt and
even the base.

ROLLED BEESWAX CANDLE

These square candles are made from the textured sheets of beeswax. They are fairly easy to make, with very little mess as only a small amount of melted wax is used.

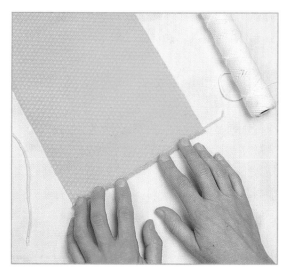

1 Lay the primed wick across the beeswax sheet and gently fold over the short edge of the beeswax to enclose it, pressing it firmly into place. Roll up the entire sheet around the wick.

TIP

Making a really neat rolled beeswax candle takes practice. Always make sure that you are rolling as tightly as possible.

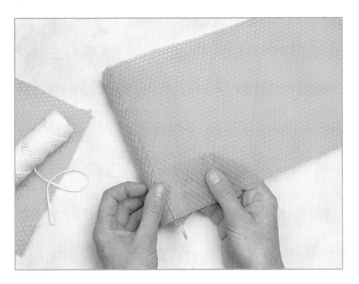

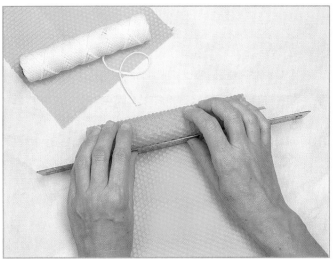

2 Place a second sheet of beeswax next to the edge of the first, and roll up tightly as in the previous step. Make sure you roll the candle evenly, so that all the edges remain at the same height.

3 Take the third sheet of beeswax. Press the metal ruler against the roll to make a sharp 90° angle and begin pressing the roll into a square shape, turning it over each time rather than rolling it.

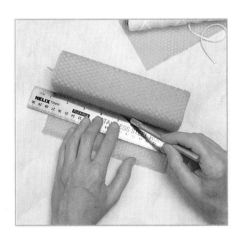

4 Continue adding sheets, using the ruler at each turn to form the sides. Once the edges are defined, score the sheet against the ruler before you roll it. This will help to make sharp corners, but take care not to cut all the way through the wax sheet.

5 When all the sheets have been used, press the end of the last sheet very firmly into the candle to make sure it does not unravel.

6 Spoon a little molten beeswax on to the base of the candle to seal all the layers.

STACKED CANDLE

This striking spiral-stacked candle makes an unusual gift. It is very quick and easy to make and no mould is required. The brilliant white texture is produced by adding a large amount of stearin to the wax mixture.

1 Cut the paper to the same width as the shortest side of the baking tray. Fold it into three lengthwise. Heat the wax and stearin together to 82°C (180°F), pour into the baking tray and leave it to cool to a soft, pliable consistency. Using the folded paper as a guide, mark the edge of the wax at the folds. Repeat at the other end. Using the same piece of paper as a guide, mark the longer sides at the same evenly spaced intervals.

YOU WILL NEED

A square-sided baking tray
Sheet of paper slightly larger than the baking tray
Scalpel or craft knife
150 g (5 oz) wax
150 g (5 oz) stearin
Wax thermometer
Metal ruler
Sharp object, such as a skewer or wicking needle
Wick sustainer
30 cm (12 in) length of 5 cm (2 in) primed wick
Wicking needle
Pliers

TIP

The addition of stearin not only whitens the wax but also ensures that the candle will be very long-burning.

2 Place the ruler across your marks and, using a craft knife, cut the soft wax into even squares.

3 Using a sharp object, make a hole in the centre of each square. Wait until the wax is completely cold and then remove the squares from the baking tray.

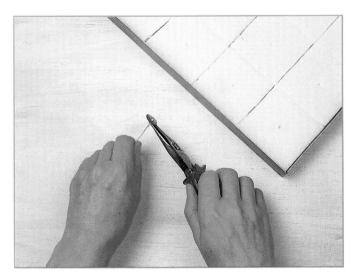

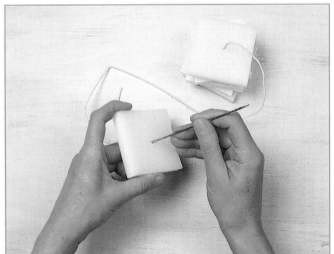

4 Using a wicking needle, thread the wick sustainer with the length of primed wick. Gently use a pair of pliers to pinch the wick sustainer to secure the wick firmly in place.

5 Thread the wick through the holes in the centre of the squares, setting the squares on top of each other at a slight angle.

NEPTUNE CANDLE

Conjure up the natural beauty of the sea by combining shells and undyed natural paraffin wax in this simple but effective candle. If you are making it as a gift, wrap the finished candle in clear cellophane and tie with a raffia bow. Other flammable objects, for example fresh or dried flowers and herbs, could also be used for a different effect.

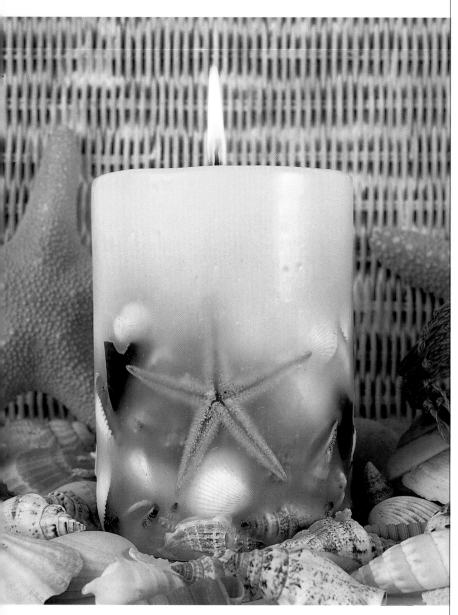

1 Have the prepared mould ready. Fix the wick but leave it hanging free over the side of the mould. Put the paraffin wax and stearin together in a double saucepan and heat to 82°C (180°F). Pour the wax mix into the mould.

SAFETY TIP

For extra safety when decorating with flammable materials such as dried flowers or herbs, put the wick in so that it reaches only halfway down the mould so that the candle will not burn below the point where the embedded decoration starts.

TIP

When adding the wax in step 5, it must be cooler than the wax already in the mould or it will melt it and the shells will fall off.

2 Wait for about 3-5 minutes until the wax has formed a skin about 1 cm (½ in) thick. Starting about 1 cm (½ in) from the edge and working quickly, cut off a 'lid' of skin from the top of the mould.

3 Pour the wax mixture back into the double saucepan with the wax disk. Clean the rim of the mould, if necessary.

4 Gently press shells into the thin layer of wax on the sides of the mould. Make sure they are embedded deeply enough to be seen from outside, taking care not to let them break through the outer surface of the wax.

5 Fix the wick in position in the usual way. Check the temperature of the hot wax and wait until it has cooled to about 73°C (165°F). Cool rapidly, if necessary by adding unmelted wax. Pour the hot wax into the mould up to the original level. Top up, allow to cool for 3-4 hours, then remove from the mould in the usual way.

LANTERN CANDLE WITH DRIED FRUITS

A wonderful, everlasting gift, this unique wax lantern would make a welcome decoration in any home. The warm colours of the dried fruit embedded in the sides glow warmly when a candle is placed inside the lantern and lit.

1 Cut the fruit into slices and place on a baking tray in a very low oven for about 1½ hours. Remove and lay out on a plate ready for use.

TIP

The same method can be used for embedding other objects. Experiment with small shells or dried herbs, or study the gallery on pages 50-51 for inspiration.

2 Heat the wax to a temperature of 82°C (180°F) and carefully pour it into the container.

3 Wait until it has cooled sufficiently for a layer of wax about 5 mm (¼ in) to have formed on the surface. Using a craft knife, cut a square about 1 cm (¾ in) from the edge of the candle and then remove the cut out square from the wax using a kitchen spatula.

4 Pour out the excess molten wax from the container into a bowl and set aside for use in step 6.

5 Take a piece of fruit and press it firmly into the wax. Repeat with all the fruit and the parsley leaves. You will have to work quite quickly. You will probably have about seven minutes before the wax is too hard.

6 Pour in wax again to just below the edge of the candle. Wait until a layer about 3 mm (⅛ in) has set, and then cut out the top and pour away the wax as you did in step 3.

7 Place a nightlight or a small scented candle in a glass container into the base of the candle and light.

APPLIQUED CANDLE

This intricately designed candle shows the versatility and ease of appliqué wax. A base colour is first wrapped around the candle, then a delicate pattern is cut out of the sheet wax and pressed down. The final touch of thin gold strips produces a sophisticated candle.

1 Wrap a piece of paper around the candle and mark where it meets with a pencil. Open out the paper and measure from the edge of the paper to the pencil mark. This is the size of the candle's circumference.

YOU WILL NEED

23 x 5 cm (9 x 2 in) church candle
Sheet of paper
Pencil
Ruler
Scissors
2 sheets of silver appliqué wax
Cutting board
Scalpel or craft knife
Graph paper
Biro
Tracing paper
Template (see page 77)
2 sheets of multi-colour appliqué wax
1 sheet of gold appliqué wax

— **T I P** —

Appliqué wax is very easy to use. It is very effective when you want to make personalised candles or candles for special occasions.

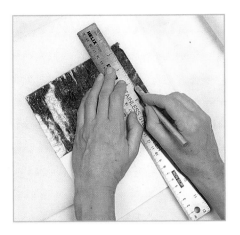

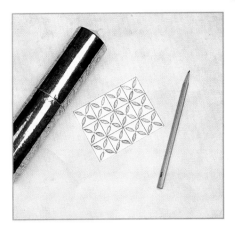

2 Place the sheets of silver appliqué wax on the cutting board and cut out two pieces of wax exactly the length of the candle's circumference. (You need to use two sheets of wax as a single sheet will not be large enough to wrap around a candle of this size.)

3 Wrap the two lengths of appliqué wax firmly around the candle. If they do not quite fill the length of the candle, use the offcut around the base.

4 Divide a piece of graph paper up into 2.5 cm (1 in) squares. Draw a diagonal across each square. Then draw a petal shape on each diagonal. Using a soft pencil draw around the petal shapes again. This template is shown in detail on page 77.

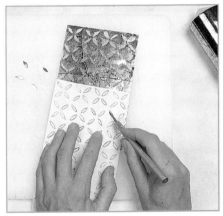

5 Turn the graph paper upside down and place on top of the tracing paper. Pressing hard, use a biro to transfer the petal shapes on to the tracing paper.

6 Using the template, cut out two sheets of multi-coloured appliqué wax. Place the sheets on the cutting board and lay the tracing paper over the sheets. Cut out the petal shapes using a craft knife.

7 Next, carefully place these cut multi-coloured sheets around the candle, as you did in step 3.

8 Cut the sheet of gold appliqué wax into very thin strips. Lay them vertically down the candle between the petal patterns. Then repeat to lay the strips horizontally around the candle, forming squares.

STENCILLED CANDLE

Stencilling is one of the easiest ways of decorating a simple candle and giving it an added finish. This project shows how to produce an attractive design using paper as a stencil.

1 Holding the candle by the wick, dip it into a dipping can of mint green wax.

YOU WILL NEED

A plain candle
A dipping can
500 gm (1 lb 1½ oz) mint green overdipping wax, heated to 79°C (175°F)
A sheet of paper
Scissors
Silver rub-on paint
Template, optional (see page 77)

TIP

Use this method for making personalised candles for special occasions, such as gold hearts on red candles for Valentines' Day or personalised wedding candles with gold paint on white wax.

VARIATIONS

If you wish, you could use a pre-cut paper doily wrapped around a candle for a pretty paint effect.

2 Fold the sheet of paper in half and make three long triangular cuts along the folded edge.

3 Fold over another 1 cm (½ in) of the paper lengthways. Make three triangular cuts just below the thickest part of each of the first cuts.

4 Then cut three small slithers off the gaps in between the triangles and open out the paper. If you find this cutting difficult, use the template on page 77 and simply trace the design on to a flat piece of paper.

5 Place the paper around the candle and hold tightly in place. Using your finger, rub the silver paste over the holes in the paper, making sure that you get the paste right into the edges. Leaving time for the paste to dry between each application, repeat four times until the candle is complete.

SNOWBALL CANDLE

Whipped wax is used here to create the realistic snow-like surface on this Christmas candle. Whip the wax just as you would an egg white. The resulting consistency resembles the texture of snow.

1 Set up a round candle mould, leaving about 5 cm (2 in) of extra wick at the base. Pour in the wax and stearin mix. Top up and allow to cool, then remove from the mould.

YOU WILL NEED

500 g (1 lb 1½ oz) white wax with 20 per cent stearin added, heated to 82°C (180°F)
Round candle mould
20 cm (8 in) length of 4 cm (1½ in) primed wick
Fork
Baking tray

TIP

If you allow the whipped wax to cool until it is almost set, you can mould whipped wax with your hands. Children love hand-moulding their own snowball candles just as they would real snow.

2 Heat the remainder of the wax to 18°C (65°F) or until it has melted, then wait until it has cooled so that skin 5 mm (¼ in) thick has formed over the surface. Using a fork, beat the wax until it has reached a soft, snow-like consistency.

3 Hold the candle in one hand and, using the fork, begin to smear the whipped wax over the candle.

4 Continue forking over the wax until a thick layer has been built up all over the candle.

5 Place the candle in a baking tray and, using a fork, make sure the wax has been applied as evenly as possible all round. Leave the candle on the tray to cool.

CHRISTMAS GALLERY

GOLD CHRISTMAS CANDLE

This is a simple and elegant candle ideal for a traditional Christmas centrepiece. Using micro soft makes it easier to serrate the surface of the candle, and the application of rub-on gold enhances the pattern inscribed by the zest peeler.

1 Heat the ivory wax to 79°C (175°F) and add the micro soft. Pour the ivory wax and the micro soft into a dipping can. Holding the candle by the wick, dip it three times.

YOU WILL NEED

A ready-made candle
2 kg (4½ lb) ivory paraffin wax
20 g (¾ oz) micro soft
Dipping can
Zest peeler
Rub-on gold wax paint

TIP

If you wish, you could use a lino cutting tool to create different patterns on the side on the candle.

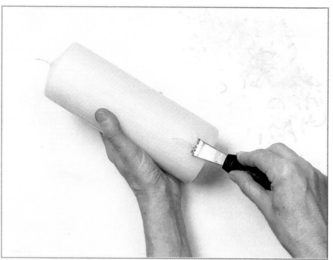

2 Pour the remaining wax into a container for future use. Fill the dipping can with cold water and dip the candle once again.

3 Wait until the wax has cooled so it is just slightly warm to the touch. Press the zest peeler firmly against the side of the candle and score a line down the side of the candle. Repeat until you have gone right around the candle.

4 Smear a little gold wax paint on your finger. Gently rub the raised surface of the candle with the gold. Continue until you are half-way around the candle.

5 Leave the candle to dry for at least two hours, and then continue around the undecorated side of the candle until all the raised surface is covered with gold. Leave to dry.

GARDEN FLARE

*These pretty garden flares will brighten
any barbecue. The lily design adds
interest and makes these flares exciting
as well as functional. Always stick the
flare securely into the ground, well away
from any inflammable surroundings,
such as leaves or wooden fences.*

1 Wrap the bandage tightly around the top
20 cm (8 in) of the bamboo stick, pulling it
out at the top so that the top 2 cm (¾ in)
protrudes beyond the bamboo.

TIP

It is essential to use rag or bandage for making garden flares as
they act as a wick. If you do not wish to use the petal shape,
simply pour more wax over the bandage. The thicker the wax layer,
the longer the flare will burn.

2 Heat the green wax to 73°C (165°F). Hold the covered bamboo stick over the saucepan and ladle wax over the first 15 cm (6 in) of the bandaged end. Keep pouring over the wax until the bandage is completely covered.

3 Push the length of wick into the top of the bandage. Heat the pink wax to 73°C (165°F). Hold the bamboo stick over the saucepan and ladle wax over the remaining exposed bandage.

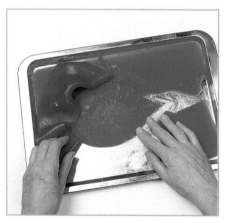

4 Using the template on page 76, cut out a piece of paper to the correct size. Heat the purple wax and micro soft mix to 82°C (180°F) and pour into the baking tray. Wait until the wax has set to a soft 'fudge' consistency. Place the petal-shaped paper on it and cut around it with a craft knife.

5 Remove the paper template. Peel away the unwanted wax around the petal on the baking tray.

6 Lift the petal shape from the baking tray and carefully fold it around the top of the bamboo stick. Place the flare in a bucket of water to cool and set the wax.

FLOATING LILY

Floating candles are always pretty and this vibrantly coloured and unusually large candle will grace any candle bowl. The shaped outer layer is made possible by the use of micro soft which keeps the wax soft for long enough for it to be shaped.

1 Pour the lime green wax into a baking tray and wait until it is almost set (i.e. warm but still soft to the touch). Using a bowl or plate as a template, cut out a circle in the middle of the wax with a craft knife.

2 Gently pull away the wax from around the circle. Carefully lift the remaining circle on to a cutting board.

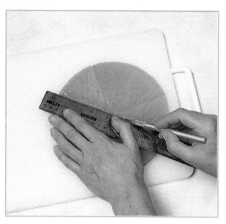

3 Using the craft knife, divide the circle into eight portions. Do not cut into the middle of the circle – leave an uncut circle with a diameter of approximately 2 cm (¾ in) in the centre.

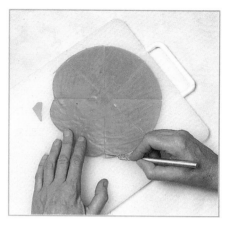

4 Using the craft knife, neatly shape the top of each of the eight segments into a scallop shape.

5 Lift up the wax from the cutting board and place into a small bowl. Place each segment so that it slightly overlaps the neighbouring segment.

6 Using a spoon, smear some green wax around the inside of the wax bowl to hold the segments in place, making sure that any holes are sealed.

7 Pour in the pink wax to within 2 mm (⅛ in) of the top.

8 Wait until the wax is almost set and press in the primed wick.

9 Resting the wick on a stick for support, carefully top up the lily with orange wax.

FLOATING HEARTS

We have used three sizes of biscuit cutter to form the shape of these delicate, yet easy-to-make candles. Sitting in a shallow glass bowl filled with water, they make a lovely centrepiece for a dinner table.

1 Pour the hot purple wax into baking tray to a depth of about 6 mm (¼ in). Press the heart-shaped biscuit moulds into the wax and leave them there.

YOU WILL NEED

Shallow baking tray
Set of 3 heart-shaped biscuit cutters
50 g (2 oz) purple wax, heated to 82°C (180°F)
150 g (6 oz) pink wax, heated to 82°C (180°F)
Length of 2.5 cm (1 in) primed wick
Skewer or wicking needle

TIP

There is now a wide range of biscuit cutters available in cooks' shops and department stores, so experiment with different shapes.

2 Carefully pour the hot pink wax into the three heart moulds, filling them up to their rims.

3 Make a hole in the centre of each heart, using a skewer or wicking needle. Push a short length of primed wick into each hole.

4 Top up each mould with more hot pink wax. Make sure the wicks are still positioned in the centre of each candle. Leave to cool.

5 When the wax is completely cold, push the pink hearts out of the moulds. The purple wax can be re-used for other candles.

FLOATING CANDLES GALLERY

CARVED TAPER CANDLES

These unusual candles have been carved into eye-catching designs. They are made using special dip-and-carve wax which will not crack or splinter during carving.

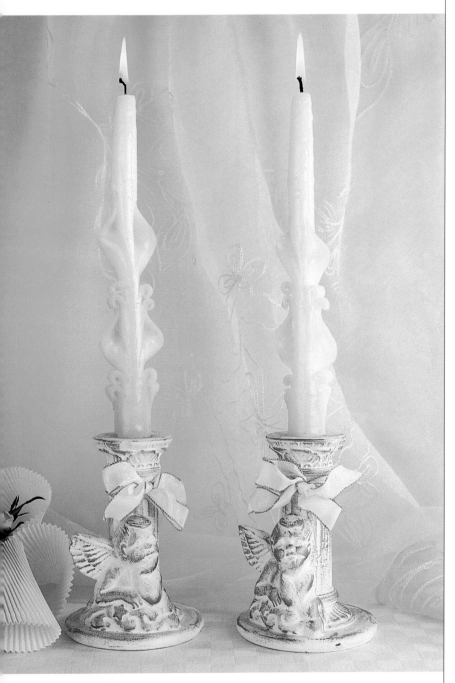

1 Heat both dipping cans to 77°C (170°F). Hold the candle in the white wax for about three minutes, or until it is slightly soft.

YOU WILL NEED

A tapered candle

A dipping can with 2 kg (4½ lb) white dip and carve wax

A dipping can with 2 kg (4½ lb) ivory dip and carve wax

Wax thermometer

Sharp knife

Old candlestick

Candle varnish and brush

TIP

It is much easier to make dip and carve candles in warm conditions. Whilst learning this technique, fix a light close to your work surface. The warmth from the light will give you precious extra seconds before the candle cools.

2 Next, dip the candle three times into ivory wax dipping can.

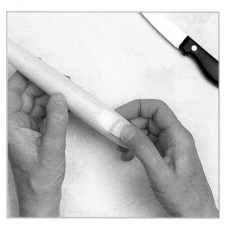

3 Using a sharp knife, make a cut 3 mm (⅛ in) deep 4 cm (1½ in) above the base of the candle. Pinch with your fingers, and gently fold back.

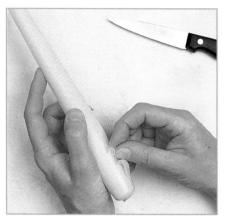

4 Make a second cut immediately above the one you have just made and roll it up above the first cut.

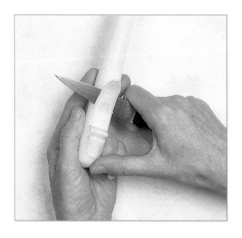

5 Make a cut 5 cm (2 in) long, finishing just below the wax you have just rolled.

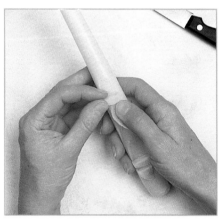

6 Carefully twist the flap around and push it firmly against the side of the candle.

7 Next, make a further cut and roll it up as before. Then make one more cut just above it.

8 Cut another 5 cm (2 in) flap (as in step 5), twist it and place it gently back onto the candle.

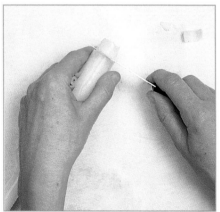

9 Repeat the design on the opposite side of the candle, then cut across the bottom of the candle to give it an even base.

10 Sit the candle in an old candlestick or fashion a support out of thick card, then give the candle a coat of varnish.

TEMPLATES

The templates shown here are smaller than required for the projects. They may be easily enlarged to the correct size on a photocopier set at 111%.

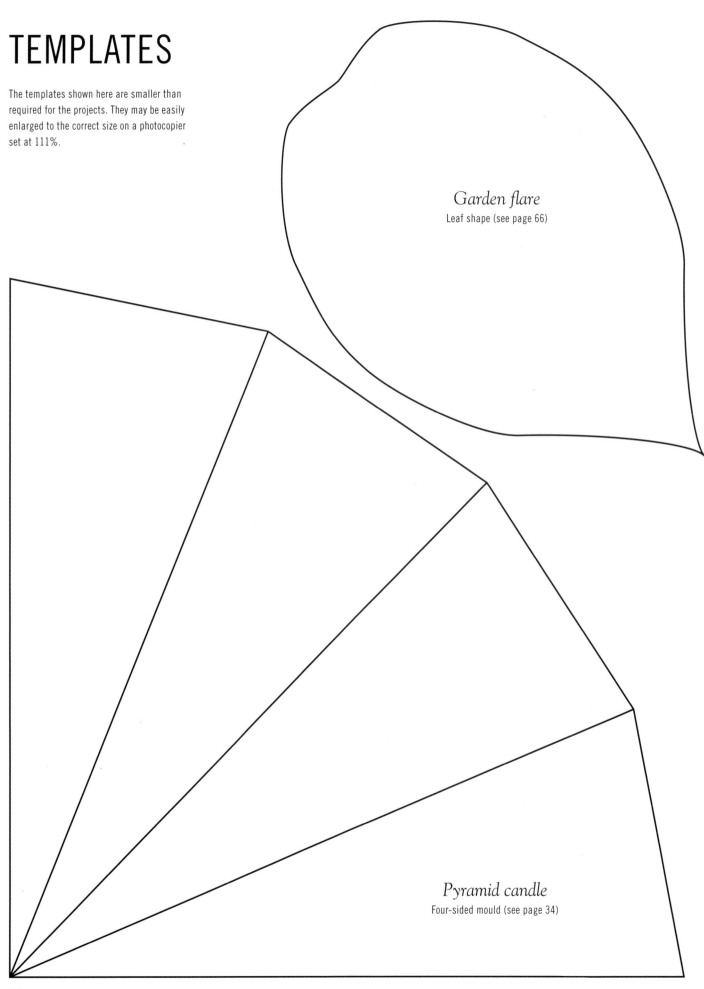

Garden flare
Leaf shape (see page 66)

Pyramid candle
Four-sided mould (see page 34)

Appliquéd candle
Repeat pattern (see page 54)

Stencilled candle
Repeat pattern (see page 58)

SUPPLIERS

UNITED KINGDOM

The Candle Shop
50 New Kings Road
London SW6 4LS
Tel: (0171) 736 0740
(*Mail order*)

and

30 The Market
Covent Garden
London WC2E 8RE
Tel: (0171) 836 9815

Panduro Hobby
Westway House
Transport Avenue
Brentford
Middlesex TW8 9HF
Tel: (0181) 847 6161
Fax: (0181) 847 5073
Orders: 01392 427788
(*Mail order catalogue*)

NEW ZEALAND

Aglow Wax & Wix
Box 7000
Auckland
Tel: (09) 834 6000

National Candles Ltd
PO Box 6024
Wellington
Tel: (04) 384 6806

Waxglo House
PO Box 19800
Christchurch
Tel: (09) 410 4727 (Auckland)
Fax: (03) 084 4777

Handcraft Supplies NZ Ltd
13-19 Rosebank Road
Avondale
Tel: (09) 828 9834

AUSTRALIA

Stacks of Wax
196 Harris Street
Pyrmont
NSW 2009
Tel: (02) 9660 0017

Pacific Petroleaum Products
1628 Ipswich Road
Rocklea
QLD 4106
Tel: (07) 3274 3140

The Wizard of the Wick
Candle Co.
(candle making classes)
40 Trinder Road
Ashgrove
QLD 4060
Tel: (07) 3366 7003

Complete Candle Supplies
Shop 3, 401 Grange Road
Findon
SA 5023
Tel: (08) 8235 1434

Norton Olympia Waxes
9 Francis Street
Wingfield
SA 5013
Tel: (07) 8347 2525

Norton Olympia Waxes
46 Renver Road
Clayton North
VIC 3168
Tel: (03) 945 6333

Gift Ware Agencies
1 Tandy Cart
Duncraig
WA 6023
Tel: (09) 9246 9445

SOUTH AFRICA

Cape Town
Crafty Suppliers
32 Main Road
Claremont 7700
Tel: (021) 61 0286

George
Art, Craft & Hobbies
72 Hibernia Street
George 6529
Tel/Fax: (0448) 74 1337

Durban
Art, Leather & Handcraft
Maple Road
Morningside
Durban 4001
Tel/Fax: (031) 23 7948

Johannesburg
Southern Arts & Crafts
105 Main Street
Rosettenville 2130
Tel/Fax: (011) 683 6566

ACKNOWLEDGEMENTS

Candles splashed with crystalline wax (pages 6 and 18): Candid Candles
Candle dipped into ice-cold water (page 19): William Watson
Refillable candle (page 21): Ken Parsons of Spectrawax
Beeswax candle (page 32): Peter Kemble
Flower embedded candles (pages 50-51): Wang International
Appliquéd candle (page 54): Jessica Payne
Pearl appliquéd candle (pages 56): Russ Berrie Ltd
Holly and berry candle (page 62): Kopschitz
Rolled candle and large floating flower (front cover): Martin Ridley